SMART WORDS
— READER —
Migration

Judith Bauer Stamper

SCHOLASTIC INC.

ISBN 978-0-545-73216-1

Photos ©: cover: Charles Kogod/Minden Pictures; 1: Ann & Steve Toon/Nature Picture Library; 2 -3: Ophir Michaeli/Moment/Getty Images; 4 -5: Flip Nicklin/Minden Pictures; 5 top: Tony Brindley/Shutterstock; 5 center: Sigrid Olsson/Photoshot; 5 bottom: Christopher Swann/Science Source; 6 -7: Bryan and Cherry Alexander/Science Source; 6: Bryan and Cherry Alexander/Nature Picture Library; 8 -9 background: Inaki Relanzon/Nature Picture Library; 8: Anup Shah/Minden Pictures; 9: Anup Shah/Visuals Unlimited; 10 -11 background: Gregory G. Dimijian, M.D./Science Source; 10: Solvin Zankl/Nature Picture Library; 11: Rainer Lesniewski/Shutterstock, Inc.; 12: Nico Tondini/Robert Harding World Imagery/Getty Images; 13: Jurgen Freund/Nature Picture Library; 14: Suzi Eszterhas/Minden Pictures; 15: The Regents of the University of California/Birch Aquarium at Scripps Institution of Oceanography, UC San Diego. All Rights Reserved; 16: Tier Und Naturfotografie J und C Sohns/Photographer's Choice/Getty Images; 16 - 17 background: Matthias Breiter/Minden Pictures; 18: Mauricio Handler/National Geographic/Getty Images; 18 -19: irin717/ iStockphoto; 20 bottom: Mark Carwardine/Visuals Unlimited, Inc.; 21: Christian Darkin/Science Source; 22 -23: Fuse/Thinkstock; 23: Mike Hollingshead/Science Source; 24 -25: Frans Lanting/Photoshot; 26: Pengranger/Thinkstock; 27 top left: Carsten Egevang/Greeland Institute of Natural Resources; 27 center right: Dean Conger/National Geographic Creative; 28: Dan Guravich/SPL/Science Source; 29: Markus Varesvuo/Nature Picture Library; 30 -31: AlbertoLoyo/Thinkstock; 32 top: Jean-Paul Ferrero/Auscape/ Biosphoto; 32 bottom: Mike Hollingshead/Science Source; back cover: Ann & Steve Toon/ Nature Picture Library.

12 11 10 9 8 7 6 5 4 3 2 1   14 15 16 17 18 19/0
Printed in the U.S.A. 40

First printing, September 2014

Designed by Lizzy Yoder

Table of Contents

Animals on the Move

All over the world, millions of animals are on the move. They thunder across the land in huge herds. They swim across vast oceans in the sea. They wing their way across continents through the air.

Why are so many animals always moving from one place to another? To survive, animals need food and water. They also need a safe place to live and have their young. To find that place, animals often have to move on, or migrate.

Migration is the large-scale movement of an animal species from one place to another. It is a kind of adaptation, or change, that helps animals survive. Migration is called a behavioral adaptation because it has to do with how animals behave, or act.

Animals that migrate are survivors. They pass down their migration routes from one generation to another. A young animal is born with the instinct to migrate. Like its ancestors, it stays on the move to survive.

Amazing Animal Migrations

In the Air — — — — — — →
Animal: Arctic Tern
Migration: 44,000 miles
(70,811 km) each year

On Land — — — — — — →
Animal: Porcupine Caribou
Migration: up to 3,000
miles (4,828 km) each year

Under the Sea — — — — →
Animal: Gray Whale
Migration: 12,000 miles
(19,312 km) each year

How many miles do you travel to get to school? To visit a grandparent? Chances are, most animals migrate much, much farther!

SMART WORDS

adaptation: a change over time to better survive in an environment

behavior: what an animal does or how it acts

instinct: behavior that is inborn rather than learned

migration: the large-scale movement of an animal species from one place to another

Chapter 1

On the Land

What animal holds the land record for longest migration? It's the caribou — also known as reindeer. Caribou live in one of the coldest places on Earth, the Arctic **tundra**.

The Sami people of Scandinavia have herded reindeer for hundreds of years.

Herds of caribou roam across the northern regions of Asia, Europe, Greenland, and North America.

During the summer, the caribou graze on plants that grow in the far north. An adult caribou can eat about 12 pounds (5.4 km) of food a day. But when winter arrives, food becomes scarce.

The first snow sends a message to the caribou — head south! They travel in huge herds across the tundra to their warmer winter homes. In all the Arctic regions, nearly 3 million caribou are on the move.

When summer arrives again, the caribou head back north. What kind of caribou migrate the farthest? It's the Porcupine Caribou herd of Canada. They complete a round-trip, **seasonal** migration of up to 3,000 miles (4,828 km) over land. That's a world record!

SMART WORDS

seasonal: having to do with the four natural parts of the year: winter, spring, summer, and fall

tundra: a cold area without trees where the soil under the surface of the ground is always frozen

A Wild Trip

The Serengeti is a huge plain that stretches across the African countries of Kenya and Tanzania. It is home to zebras, wildebeest, gazelles, lions, and many other African animals. It is also home to one of the most awesome migrations on Earth.

The Serengeti has seasons that **alternate** between dry and rainy. To survive, many animals have to stay on the move — to follow the rain and the food it provides. Millions make this 1,000 to 1,800 mile (1,609–2,897 km) journey each year, including giant herds of wildebeest.

Wildebeest thunder across the Serengeti.

From December to March, the wildebeest graze on grasses in the southeastern part of the Serengeti. After a few months, the herds follow the rain to the west and then the north. In August, they reach the Mara River. There is fresh grass on the other side of the river. But the animals must risk their lives to reach it.

The Mara is full of crocodiles. The crocodiles devour many of the slower, weaker wildebeests. Others drown in the river's strong current. Still more die in the wild stampede of thousands of animals. The animals that get across the Mara survive—to make the journey again another year.

SMART WORD

alternate: to take turns

On the March

Deep in the rain forest of Costa Rica, hungry army ants are on the march. Why are they called army ants? Because they travel in armies of up to 1 million ants! These killer ants eat everything in their way — ants, insects, lizards, spiders, and even snakes!

Army ants are always looking for food. When they have eaten everything in one place, they move to another. Every three weeks they are on the march. The huge colonies of ants migrate from place to place in huge swarms at night.

A huge swarm of army ants can be 40 feet (12 m) wide and up to 200 feet (60 m) long.

Army ants have giant hooked jaws to devour their victims.

In their march to survive, the ants travel up to nine miles a year. That doesn't sound like much compared to other land migrations. But ants are tiny insects. In one night, they march a distance that equals a human running a marathon!

Use your SMART WORDS

Answer each question with a Smart Word.

adaptation alternate behavioral colony

instinct migration seasonal tundra

1. What behavior is inborn rather than learned?

2. To _____ is to take turns.

3. What is a change over time to better survive in an environment?

4. The soil under the surface of the ground in this area is always frozen.

5. What do you call a large group of animals living together?

6. What kind of adaptation describes how an animal acts, as opposed to looks?

7. This describes the four natural parts of the year.

8. _____ is the large-scale movement of an animal species from one place to another.

Answers on page 32

Talk Like a Scientist

Look at the photograph. Use your Smart Words to describe what it shows.

SMART FACTS

Did You Know?

Red crabs go on the march each year on tiny Christmas Island in the Pacific Ocean. The crabs migrate from the rain forests to the beach. Fifty million strong, they cover the island like a crawling blanket!

Thirsty Elephants

Some African elephants live near the Sahara desert. They migrate constantly to find water. In 1983, a drought dried up all their water holes. The government trucked in tons of water and saved the elephants.

That's Amazing!

A baby wildebeest can walk minutes after it's born! There's no time to waste when hungry lions are around.

Chapter 2

Under the Sea

Whale watchers sight a migrating gray whale off the coast of California.

Land animals migrate long distances. But ocean animals travel even farther! Take gray whales, for example. These huge creatures migrate 12,000 miles (19,312 km) a year. And they have a special reason for their trip. They swim to warmer waters to **reproduce,** or have babies.

Gray whales weigh 30 to 40 tons (27,200 to 36,300 kg) and grow up to 50 feet (15 m) long. During the summer, they live in the northern waters off Alaska. They eat millions of tiny sea animals to build up a thick layer of **blubber.**

In October, the days get shorter and the water gets colder. The whales begin their long journey south. Their blubber keeps them warm and gives them energy for the trip. For two months, the whales travel down the west coast of Canada, the United States, and Mexico.

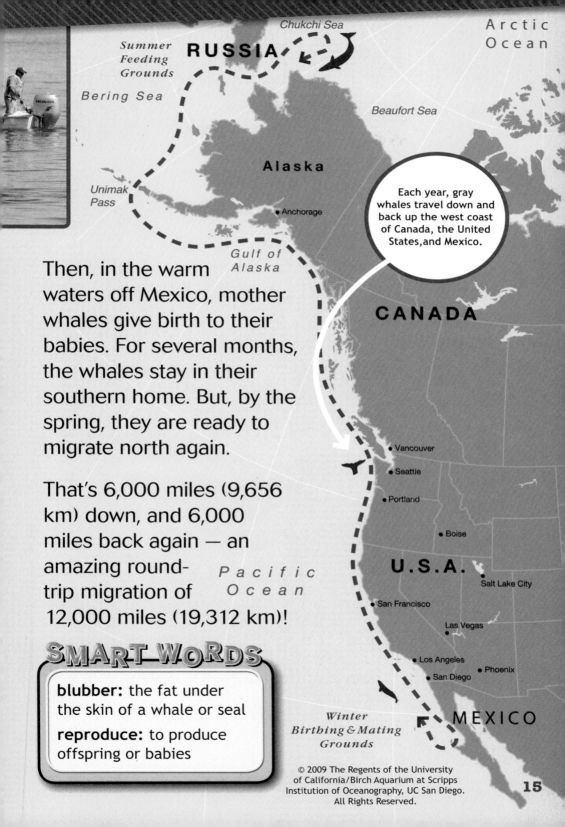

Chukchi Sea

Arctic Ocean

RUSSIA

Summer Feeding Grounds

Bering Sea

Beaufort Sea

Alaska

Unimak Pass

• Anchorage

Gulf of Alaska

Each year, gray whales travel down and back up the west coast of Canada, the United States, and Mexico.

CANADA

Then, in the warm waters off Mexico, mother whales give birth to their babies. For several months, the whales stay in their southern home. But, by the spring, they are ready to migrate north again.

That's 6,000 miles (9,656 km) down, and 6,000 miles back again — an amazing round-trip migration of 12,000 miles (19,312 km)!

• Vancouver

• Seattle

• Portland

• Boise

U.S.A.

Pacific Ocean

Salt Lake City

• San Francisco

Las Vegas

• Los Angeles

• Phoenix

• San Diego

SMART WORDS

blubber: the fat under the skin of a whale or seal

reproduce: to produce offspring or babies

Winter Birthing & Mating Grounds

MEXICO

Against the Current

Among sea animals, salmon are special. Each year, they make an amazing journey — upstream, back to the place where they were born.

Pacific salmon hatch from eggs laid in the rivers of the northwest United States. When the salmon grow to about 4 inches (10 cm) long, they migrate to the Pacific Ocean. They travel downstream, swimming tail first to the sea! For four to eight years, the salmon live in the ocean. Then their instinct sends them back up the rivers where they were born.

A brown bear catches its lunch during the salmon migration.

These salmon go airborne to swim upstream.

This migration is full of dangers. The salmon must swim upstream against the river's current. They have to jump over rocks and even waterfalls. They have to escape the paws of hungry bears. How many of the salmon survive? Only one salmon in every thousand makes it home again!

The survivors **spawn**, laying eggs in the river. Young salmon hatch and grow. For them, the journey is just beginning.

SMART WORD

spawn: to produce a large number of eggs

Amazing Turtle Trek

Whales and fish aren't the only ocean animals that migrate. So do sea turtles. The leatherback sea turtle grows up to 7 feet (2 m) long and can weigh up to 2,000 pounds (900 kg)! Not only is it the biggest sea turtle, it also makes the longest turtle migration — about 7,400 miles (11,909 km) round-trip!

Sea turtles hatch from eggs that their mothers lay on a beach. Right away, the little **hatchlings** head for the ocean and dive in. They swim far away and spend many years feeding and growing. But soon after they mate, female leatherbacks swim back to where they were born. In fact, they return to the very same beach!

Leatherback sea turtle hatchlings are only 4 inches long when they head to the sea.

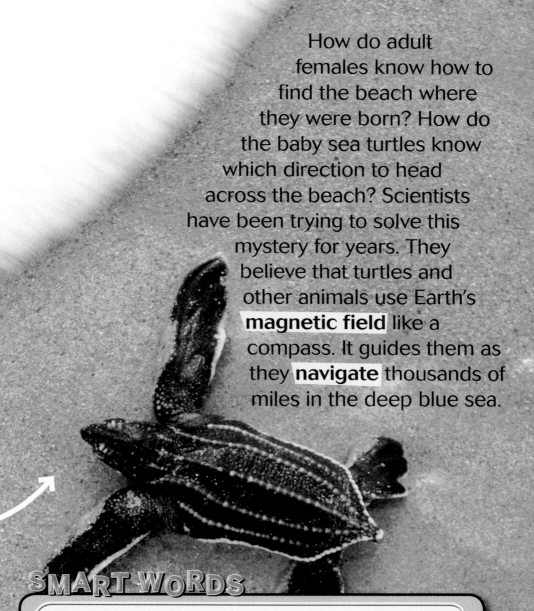

How do adult females know how to find the beach where they were born? How do the baby sea turtles know which direction to head across the beach? Scientists have been trying to solve this mystery for years. They believe that turtles and other animals use Earth's **magnetic field** like a compass. It guides them as they **navigate** thousands of miles in the deep blue sea.

SMART WORDS

hatchling: a recently hatched animal

magnetic field: lines of magnetic force that extend from the North Pole to the South Pole

navigate: to travel using a system to guide you

Use your SMART WORDS

Read each definition. Choose the correct Smart Word.

| blubber | hatchling | magnetic field |
| navigate | reproduce | spawn |

1. It means to produce offspring or babies.
    Is it **reproduce** or **navigate**?

2. A whale has a layer of this under its skin.
    Is it a **magnetic field** or **blubber**?

3. A recently hatched turtle is called this.
    Is it **spawn** or **hatchling**?

4. It means to travel using a system to guide you.
    Is it **spawn** or **navigate**?

5. It is made up of lines of magnetic force that extend from Earth's poles.
    Is it a **hatchling** or a **magnetic field**?

6. A salmon does this when it reproduces.
    Is it **spawn** or **navigate**?

Answers on page 32

Talk Like a Scientist

Make a list of three fascinating facts about ocean animals that migrate. Use your Smart Words.

SMART FACTS

Did You Know

Sperm whales are big animals with big appetites — one sperm whale can eat about one ton of fish and squid per day!

Up and Down

Some sea creatures spend the day near the ocean bottom. At night, they migrate up to find food near the surface. How do they do it? They fill their swim bladders with gassy air and float right up.

Sea Superhighway

Some sea animals catch a ride on the Gulf Stream in the Atlantic Ocean. This ocean current flows faster than the water around it. They go with the flow!

Chapter 3

In the Air

Have you ever seen a migrating animal? Try looking up to the sky in the fall. All kinds of birds are winging their way south. You might see honking geese flying in a V. You might see hawks, storks, or even eagles!

Birds are magnificent migrators. They have bodies adapted to fly long distances. They have instincts that take them on mind-boggling journeys. Even before migration begins, birds start preparing. They load up on large amounts of food energy. They build up their muscles to power their wings. Some even grow new, stronger feathers for the trip.

Birds are also excellent navigators. Their instincts, inherited from generations before them, tell them where to go. When days grow shorter and the temperature drops, they head south. Some use the position of the sun in the sky to find their way. Others use landmarks like mountains and rivers. Birds that fly at night navigate using the moon and the stars.

...ng on Thermals

...n a migrating bird catch a free ride?
...e hawks and pelicans catch a
... A **thermal** is a rising current of
...r. It lifts a bird up and lets it
...e bird doesn't even have to
...ings!

...dian geese fly
...V formation to
...energy and to
...rdinate their
...ght pattern.

SMART WORDS

landmark: an object in a landscape that can be easily seen or is important

thermal: a rising current of warm air

Millions of Monarchs

Every autumn, millions of monarch butterflies flutter up into the sky. They leave their summer homes in Canada and the United States and they head south for the winter. Their instincts seem to say, "Meet me in Mexico!"

The butterflies migrate 50 to 100 miles (80–160 km) a day. Finally, they reach the oyamel forests of Mexico. Some butterflies even find the exact tree where their ancestors landed years before.

This fir tree in the oyamel forest of Mexico is covered by monarch butterflies. The number of monarchs has been dropping in recent years.

The millions of butterflies in the forest are quite a sight. Monarchs' wings are bright orange and patterned with black veins. The entire forest looks like it is covered in orange confetti!

The monarchs are special among migrating animals. Their life cycle is short, and the trip is long. Some monarchs go through four different generations during a round-trip migration. Yet each new generation is born with the same flight path inside its tiny brain.

SMART WoRD

life cycle: the series of changes a living thing goes through from birth to death

Frequent Flier Champions!

Of all the animals in the world, which is the champion migrator? It is the tiny Arctic tern. The Arctic tern weighs in at 4 ounces (113 grams) and is only 11 inches (28 cm) long. Despite its small size, it travels about 44,000 miles (71,000 km) each year!

Where in the world does the tern fly this many miles? It migrates from one of Earth's **poles** to another — and back again. The tiny bird breeds during the summer in the Arctic, near the North Pole. Then it begins its long journey to the Antarctic, near the South Pole.

A whole colony of terns takes off together for their long flight. On the way, they stop in the Atlantic Ocean to fuel up on small fish.

The Arctic tern is small and slender, but it flies farther every year than any other bird.

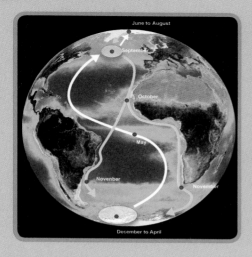

June to August

September

October

May

November

November

December to April

The birds split into two groups, but meet up again in the Antarctic. After eating from the rich feeding grounds there, they take off for their return trip to the Arctic.

How do we know the tern's flight path? Scientists **monitor** their journey with special **tracking devices**. They even know that the terns don't fly in a straight line on the way back. Instead, they zigzag back north, catching winds for a faster ride. These tiny terns have adapted to life as high fliers!

An Arctic tern is banded so scientists can track its migration.

SMART WORDS

monitor: to watch closely over a period of time

poles: the two geographical points on Earth that are farthest away from the equator

tracking device: a tiny machine planted under an animal's skin that tracks its location

Use your SMART WORDS

Match each description with the correct Smart Word.

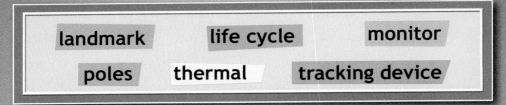

landmark   life cycle   monitor

poles   thermal   tracking device

1. an object in a landscape that can be easily seen or is important

2. a rising current of warm air

3. the series of changes a living thing goes through from birth to death

4. to watch closely over a period of time

5. a tiny machine planted under an animal's skin that records its location

6. the two geographical points on Earth that are farthest away from the equator

Answers on page 32

Talk Like a Scientist

Tell how scientists use tracking devices to learn about migration. Use your Smart Words to explain.

tracking device

SMART FACTS

Did You Know?

Birds face many dangers during migration. One danger is buildings with windows. Millions of birds die each year from window collisions.

Fastest Bird Award

The great snipe flies at speeds of up to 60 mph (96 km). That's the speed limit for cars on many highways!

Amazing!

Before they migrate, most birds pack on fat reserves. Some increase their body weight by 50 percent!

Glossary

adaptation: a change over time to better survive in an environment

alternate: to take turns

behavior: what an animal does or how it acts

blubber: the fat under the skin of a whale or seal

colony: a large group of animals that live together

hatchling: a recently hatched animal

instinct: behavior that is inborn rather than learned

landmark: an object in a landscape that can be easily seen or is important

life cycle: the series of changes a living thing goes through from birth to death

magnetic field: lines of magnetic force that extend from the North Pole to the South Pole

migration: the large-scale movement of an animal species from one place to another

monitor: to watch closely over a period of time

navigate: to travel using a system to guide you

poles: the two geographical points on Earth that are farthest away from the equator

reproduce: to produce offspring or babies

seasonal: having to do with the four natural parts of the year: winter, spring, summer, and fall

spawn: to produce a large number of eggs

thermal: a rising current of warm air

tracking device: a tiny machine planted under an animal's skin that tracks its location

tundra: a cold area without trees where the soil under the surface of the ground is always frozen.

Index

SMART WORDS Answer Key

page 12
1. instinct 2. alternate 3. adaptation 4. tundra 5. colony
6. behavioral 7. seasonal 8. migration

page 20
1. reproduce 2. blubber 3. hatchling 4. navigate 5. magnetic
   field 6. spawn

page 28
1. landmark 2. thermal 3. life cycle 4. monitor 5. tracking
   device 6. poles